101 BETS You Will ALWAYS Win

Also by Richard Wiseman

The Luck Factor

Did You Spot the Gorilla?

Quirkology

59 Seconds

Paranormality

Night School

RICHARD WISEMAN

101 BETS
You Will ALWAYS Win

Jaw-Dropping Illusions, Remarkable
Riddles, Scintillating Science Stunts,
and Cunning Conundrums
That Will Astound and Amaze
Everyone You Know

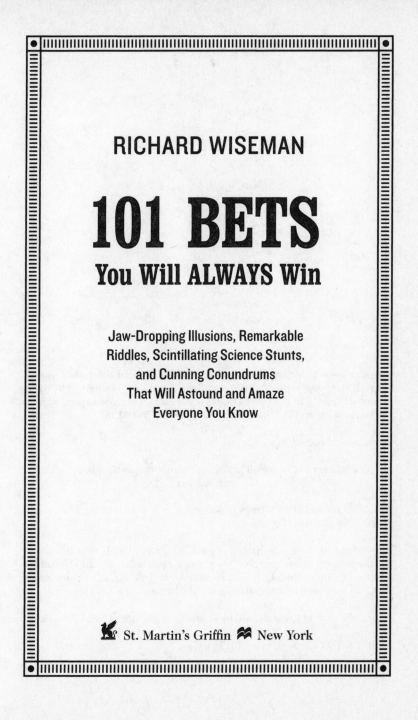 St. Martin's Griffin ❦ New York

www.stmartins.com

The Library of Congress Cataloging-in-Publication Data is available upon request.

ISBN 978-1-250-12185-1 (trade paperback)
ISBN 978-1-250-12187-5 (e-book)

Our books may be purchased in bulk for promotional, educational, or business use. Please contact your local bookseller or the Macmillan Corporate and Premium Sales Department at 1-800-221-7945, extension 5442, or by e-mail at MacmillanSpecialMarkets@macmillan.com.

First published in Great Britain by Boxtree, an imprint of Pan Macmillan

First U.S. Edition: September 2016

10 9 8 7 6 5 4 3 2 1

To Quirkology fans everywhere

CONTENTS

Let's try something right now.

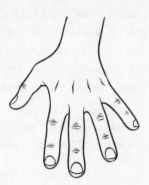

Please place your hand flat on a table.

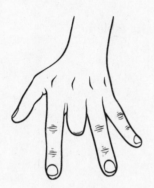

Next, bend your middle finger under your hand, so that the knuckle rests on the table like this. Perfect.

I bet that you can't lift your *third finger* up and down, and tap it on the table.

Sounds simple? No matter how hard you try, you won't be able to do it!

Congratulations, you have just carried out your very first bet, and now you can use it to amuse and amaze others.

But hold on. I can hear the more curious among you thinking, 'That's great, but why does it work?' It's an excellent question and I am glad you asked.

Your forearm muscles are connected to the bones in your fingers via tough cords of tissue called tendons. When you contract your forearm muscles the tendons tighten and your fingers move.

Your thumb, first finger and little finger each have their

own tendon, but your middle and third fingers share a tendon. When you tuck your middle finger under your hand this tendon is stretched, and so can't move your third finger.

And why do these two fingers share a tendon? Because you use them to grasp large objects, and they are more effective if they work together. In fact, scientists think that this mechanism evolved to allow our primate ancestors to hold heavy stone tools.

So now you know. A moment ago it was a fun bet. Now it illustrates a vital stage in human evolution and has changed the entire course of history.

Oh, and you can take your hand off the table now.

WELCOME

This book is about how to perform the impossible. For years I travelled the globe in search of the world's greatest bets and challenges. Leaving no stone unturned, I have tracked down 101 bets that appear totally impossible, yet are easy to win once you know the secret.

But there is more to these bets than impressing and entertaining your friends. They are also a gateway into serious science and fascinating facts, enabling you to impress others with your new-found knowledge of life, the universe and everything.

It's almost time to set off. Fasten your seat belt, because you are about to enter a weird world where nothing is quite as it seems. A world full of jaw-dropping stunts, scintillating science, and cunning conundrums. A world of 101 amazing bets you will always win.

Enjoy.

Richard Wiseman

BEFORE WE START

Some of the bets involve everyday objects, such as glasses, knives and matches, that could potentially be dangerous in the wrong hands. We are not responsible for any physical or financial harm that you may suffer as a result of performing the bets, so read on at your own risk! If you turn the page we'll understand you're intrepid and that's all fine with you. Oh, and if you're young of mind, make sure you are supervised by an adult whenever you carry out a bet that involves fire or sharp objects. Many thanks.

BODY MAGIC

TEN WAYS TO WIN WITH YOUR HANDS AND FEET

AMAZING FACTS ABOUT YOUR BODY

☞ Each day your heart will beat over 100,000 times.

☞ About 60 per cent of your body is made up of water.

☞ Every month your body completely replaces its outer skin.

☞ A quarter of all the bones in your body are in your feet.

☞ A matchbox-sized block of your bone can support four times more weight than concrete.

YOU NEED HANDS

For this bet, all you need to do is hold out your two hands and say, 'Counting my thumbs as fingers, how many fingers am I holding up?'

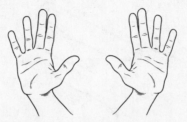

The correct answer is ten. Then say, 'So if this is ten fingers, how many fingers are there on ten hands?' Almost everyone will say 100. In fact, the correct answer is fifty!

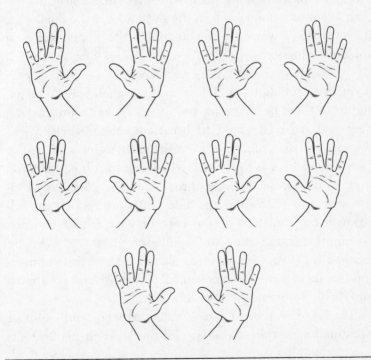

BREAK POINT

Ask your friend to hold out their hand. Next, place a matchstick across the top of their middle finger, like this.

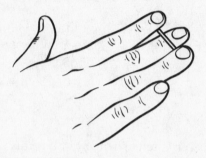

Finally, tell them that they have to break the matchstick simply by pushing down on it with their first and third fingers. It sounds simple and so they will accept the challenge. However, they won't be able to break the matchstick and you'll win the bet!

If you push the matchstick further down their middle finger, and have them bend the tops of their first and third fingers, they will easily be able to break the matchstick. Why? Because you are using your friend's fingers as levers. The key to any good lever is the distance between the object that you want to lift (or, in this case, break) and the point on which the lever tips (known as the 'fulcrum'). In this bet, the fulcrum is the knuckles at the base of your friend's fingers. Placing the match close to the fulcrum gives you a greater mechanical advantage, whereas placing it towards the fingertips results in a smaller mechanical advantage and it's almost impossible to break the match.

The famous Ancient Greek mathematician and engineer Archimedes described the laws of the lever in his 250 BCE bestseller *On the Equilibrium of Planes*, and was so certain of the power of his discovery that he famously announced, 'Give me a place to stand and with a lever I will move the whole world.' At the time no one was willing to take Archimedes up on his bold assertion, which is perhaps unfortunate because modern-day mathematicians have figured out that to win the bet, Archimedes would have required a lever with a long arm that was 1,000,000,000,000,000,000,000 times longer than the short arm!

CATCH ME IF YOU CAN

Ask your friend to hold their thumb and first finger about an inch apart, like this.

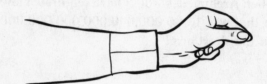

Now place a banknote in the gap between their thumb and finger.

Explain that in a moment you are going to drop the banknote and they can keep the money if they can catch it. Amazingly, they will miss the banknote every time.

You can use the same method to find out whether you have fast reactions.

1) Hold your thumb and first finger about an inch apart.

2) Ask a friend to hold a twelve-inch ruler at the top (the end nearest the twelve-inch mark) and to place the bottom of the ruler between your finger and thumb.

3) Tell your friend to wait a few moments and then suddenly drop the ruler.

4) When you see the ruler move, catch it as quickly as you can.

5) Look at where you caught the ruler and then use this table to find out your reaction time.

Inches	Reaction time in seconds
2	0.1
4	0.14
6	0.17
8	0.2
10	0.23
12	0.25

Most people catch the ruler between the six-inch and eight-inch mark, translating into a reaction time of roughly 0.17 to 0.2 seconds. If you reliably catch the ruler around the 4.5-inch mark then you have the reaction time of a professional athlete. Either that, or you cheated.

HEAD START

Place your hand flat on your head and bet your friend that they can't lift your hand off your head. It sounds simple, but it's impossible and so you will win the bet.

Why does it work? When your friend tries to lift your forearm they are also lifting your upper arm. Luckily for you, your upper arm is firmly connected to the rest of your body, and so without realizing it they are actually trying to lift your entire body weight!

INFLATION

Place five or six pennies on a table and balance another penny on its edge. Ask your friend how many pennies you will need to stack up to reach the height of the upright penny.

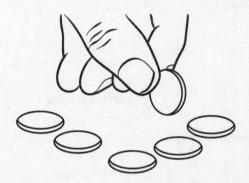

They might guess five or six. You will win the bet because the answer is an amazing twelve coins!

MAKE A GOOD FIST OF IT

Ask your friend to place one fist on top of the other. Next, take hold of their top fist with your right hand and their bottom fist with your left hand. Then move your right hand to the right and your left hand to the left and show your friend how easy it is to pull their fists apart.

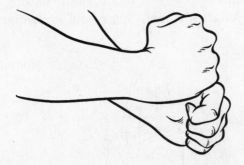

Now bet your friend that when you place *your* fists together, they will find it hard to push them apart. To win the bet you need to be a bit sneaky. When you put one fist on top of the other, secretly hold out your lower thumb and wrap your upper hand around it! That way, your friend will struggle to push your fists apart.

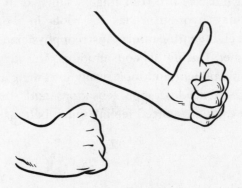

INSTANT HYPNOSIS

Bet your friend that you can move their fingers using the power of hypnosis. When they accept the bet, ask them to clasp their hands together and extend their two first fingers like this. Next, ask them to look into your eyes and count to five. Tell your friend that they are now hypnotized and ask them to imagine their two first fingers slowly moving towards one another. Amazingly, their fingers will mysteriously drift together!

This isn't really a demonstration of hypnosis. Instead, it takes considerable effort to keep your first fingers apart, and as your muscles tire your fingers slowly drift together.

Modern-day hypnotism has its roots in work of the charismatic eighteenth-century Austrian physician, Dr Franz Anton Mesmer. During his consultations, Mesmer would sit in front of his patient and look firmly into their eyes. Many patients experienced strange sensations and sudden convulsions, and then reported feeling much better.

In 1784 King Louis XVI of France asked Benjamin Franklin to investigate Mesmer. Franklin sometimes blindfolded the patients so that they didn't know when they were receiving Mesmer's magical treatment, and discovered that the patients only reported positive effects when they thought that they were being treated. As a result, Franklin concluded that Mesmer's 'cures' were all down to self-delusion.

However, Mesmer's legacy lives on because the investigation was one of the first to use 'blind' methods – which are now commonplace in science – and because his work resulted in the verb 'mesmerize', which means to amaze and astound.

Over 200 years later, scientists still can't agree on what's actually happening when people are hypnotized. Some researchers believe that hypnosis is a special state of consciousness, whilst others argue that it is an unusual type of role-playing. Either way, the good news is that the technique can be used to get people to eat an onion, act like a chicken, and shout out their bank account details.

COINING IT IN

Ask your friend to link their hands together, and then raise their first and third fingers like this.

Now place a coin between their third fingers, and bet them that they can't move their fingers apart and release the coin.

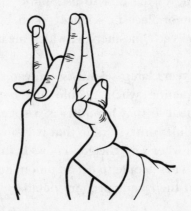

It sounds easy but it's almost impossible!

ROUND IN CIRCLES

Ask someone to sit down, cross their right leg over their left leg and rotate their right foot clockwise.

Now tell them that you can reverse the direction of their foot without touching it. To win the bet, simply ask them to draw a number '6' in the air with their right finger.

Almost everyone will automatically reverse the direction of their right foot, and you will win the bet!

The left side of your brain controls the right side of your body, and it struggles to produce two opposing movements at the same time. Try doing the same bet with your right foot and left hand and you will discover that it's much easier.

THE FLOATING SAUSAGE

Tell your friend that you can magically make a sausage float in front of their eyes. When they accept the bet, ask them to place the tips of their first fingers together, and hold their hands about six inches from their nose. Next, ask them to focus on an object in the distance. After a few moments they'll find that the ends of their fingers appear to look like a small sausage! Not only that, but when they move their fingers a few millimetres apart, the sausage will appear to float in mid-air!

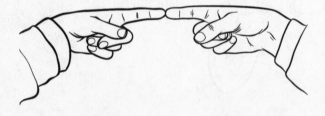

In 1927, University of Chicago psychologist W. L. Sharp first described this illusion in an academic paper entitled 'The Floating-Finger Illusion'. In this little-known paper, Sharp explained how he frequently used the illusion to evoke a sense of curiosity in his students, writing, '. . . not infrequently have I noted students blinking their eyes and shaking their heads vigorously as if to pull themselves back to reality'.

The illusion works because when you focus on a distant object each of your eyes receives a slightly different view of your fingers.

MAGNETIC FINGERS

Form your hands into fists and then hold out the first fingers of each hand. Keeping your hands close to your body, touch the ends of your first fingers together.

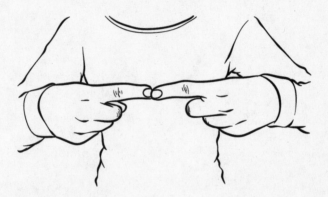

Now challenge your friend to hold your wrists and pull your fingers apart. It sounds simple but they won't be able to do it!

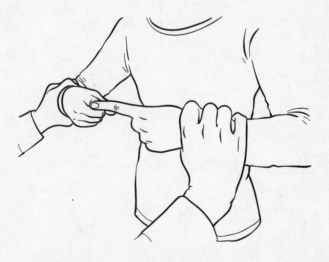

MONEY MATTERS

TEN WAYS TO WIN WITH
COINS AND NOTES

AMAZING FACTS ABOUT MONEY

☞ Banknotes first appeared in China during the Tang Dynasty (AD 618–907), more than 500 years before they were used in Europe.

☞ In times gone by, criminals shaved the edges off coins and sold the metal, and the ridges around the rims of coins were originally created to prevent such practices.

☞ It costs the American mint 1.5 cents to manufacture a one-cent coin.

☞ In 2002, researchers found faecal matter on 94 per cent of dollar bills tested. Paper money can carry more germs than a toilet, and the flu virus can live on a banknote for up to seventeen days.

☞ In 1978, Space Invaders became so popular in Japan that there was a nationwide shortage of the 100-yen coins needed to play the game.

THE BANG BANG BOTTLE

Place a banknote on a table and then balance a bottle on top of it like this.

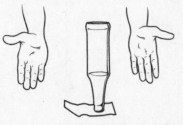

Bet your friend that you can remove the banknote without touching or knocking over the bottle. To win the bet, simply make one of your hands into a fist and hold the end of the banknote with your other hand.

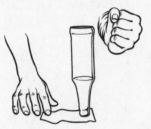

When you knock your fist on the table the bottle will jump, just a little, into the air. At that exact moment, use your other hand to slide the banknote out from under the bottle!

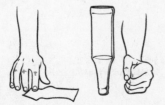

THE PENNY STACK

Place a small coin on a smooth table and then stack several larger coins on top of it.

Next, challenge your friend to remove the small coin, but without touching the larger ones. To win the bet, find another small coin and quickly flick it along the table so that it hits the small coin at the bottom of the stack. The small coin under the stack will shoot out from under the larger coins, and then you can simply pick it up!

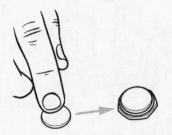

The seventeenth-century scientist Sir Isaac Newton spent much of his time watching objects move, and eventually came up with his now-famous laws of motion. The Penny Stack uses Isaac's first law, which states that stationary objects remain where they are unless a force acts on them. Isaac called this 'inertia', and he used it to explain why people struggle to get out of a warm bed on a winter's morning (I made that last bit up). The small coin shoots out of the stack because of the force delivered during the collision. However, the other coins in the stack remain where they are because of their inertia, and simply drop down onto the coin that was flicked along the table.

Although Newton is best known for his scientific achievements, he was also a lifelong alchemist and spent much of his time searching for the philosopher's stone – a legendary substance thought to have the power to transform lead into gold. Unfortunately, this work was literally to be the death of him. Newton's alchemical pursuits involved distilling mercury, and a recent analysis of his hair samples revealed very high levels of this dangerous chemical, suggesting that Newton may have died from mercury poisoning.

A BRIDGING LOAN

Place a banknote on the table and tell your friend that they can have the money if they win the bet. Next, place two large glasses, a smaller glass and some matches on the table. Now challenge your friend to use the objects on the table to support the smaller glass between the larger glasses.

In fact, the matches are just decoys, and to win the bet you have to use the banknote! Simply accordion-pleat the banknote along its length, place it between the larger glasses like a bridge, stand the smaller glass on top of the banknote, and you have won the bet.

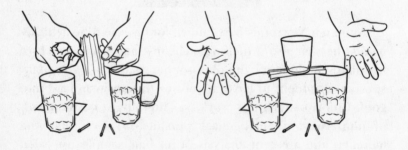

The banknote supports the weight of the glass because the pleating increases its strength. The same idea was used in one of the world's greatest inventions – the corrugated cardboard box. This amazing creation dates back to 1856, when English top hat salesman Edward Allen wanted to keep his hats in shape. Inspired by sixteenth-century ruffled lace collars, Allen created pleated paper and placed it inside his hats.

In 1871, New Yorker Albert Jones obtained an American patent for the same idea, and within a few years other inventors had increased the strength of the pleated paper even further by gluing it between two sheets of cardboard. Around the turn of the last century the first corrugated cardboard boxes began to roll off American production lines. The manufacturers quickly realized that they had nothing to pack the boxes in and so started to produce even bigger boxes. Over the years the rapid rise in shipped goods has created a near insatiable need for boxes, with some economists arguing that the global economy simply couldn't thrive without the corrugated cardboard box. And all because a man once wanted to keep his top hats in tip-top condition.

THE COIN SLIDE

Balance two coins on the edge of a glass and challenge your friend to lift the glass. Oh, and they are only allowed to touch the coins!

To win the bet, place your first finger and thumb on the coins, quickly move them down the sides of the glass, and then you can lift up the glass holding just the coins.

LIVING ON THE EDGE

Challenge your friend to balance a small coin on the edge of a banknote. When they give up, first fold the banknote into a 'V' shape and balance the coin on the 'V'.

Next, slowly pull the ends of the banknote. Amazingly, the coin will end up balanced on the edge of the banknote!

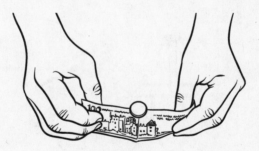

This bet is much easier if you use a crisp, fresh note.

When you pull the ends of the note, take your time and don't sneeze.

I'LL HUFF AND I'LL PUFF

Place a playing card on a glass, put a tube of paper on the playing card, and finally balance a coin on top of the tube. Now challenge your friend to move the coin into the glass, but without touching the playing card, the tube or the coin.

When your friend gives up, simply blow upwards under the playing card – the tube and the playing card will fly away and the coin will drop into the glass.

IN CREDIT

Pour some water into a glass and then balance a credit card on the edge of the glass like this. Next, challenge your friend to balance some coins on the overhanging end of the credit card.

They will fail because the credit card will fall off the glass. To win the bet, completely fill the glass with water and then place the credit card on top of the glass. The credit card will stick to the surface of the water and you will find that you can place several coins on the overhanging end of the credit card.

Water molecules are attracted to one another. However, the molecules on the surface of the water have air above them and so have fewer molecules to cling to. As a result, they develop especially strong bonds with the other molecules around them, and the resulting cohesion creates surface tension. When the credit card is first placed on the water it rests on top because of this surface tension. Then, when the credit card and water come into contact, the two very different types of molecules are attracted to one another and this adhesion stops the credit card moving away from the water.

GETTING DICEY

Place a coin between two dice like this.

Hand your friend a pen, and challenge them to use the pen to remove the coin and leave the dice stacked. However, they are only allowed to touch the coin with the pen. When they give up, press the button on the top of the pen, but don't release it. Next, place the end of the button close to the edge of the coin. Finally, release the button! It will spring out and knock the coin out from between the dice.

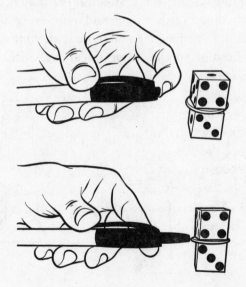

JUST ONE FINGER

Place a banknote on the top of a bottle and then place some coins on top of the banknote like this.

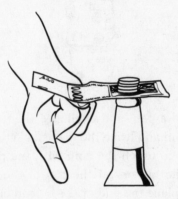

Challenge your friend to remove the note but leave the coins in place, and explain that they can only use one finger. The secret is simple. Lick your first finger so that it has some saliva on it. Next, raise your hand and, as you bring it down, strike the overhanging banknote with your finger. The banknote will stick to the licked finger and whip out from beneath the coins.

Why do you have to lick your finger for the bet to work? Your body naturally produces oils that prevent your skin from drying out. This oil makes your fingers relatively smooth, and so during the bet you run the risk of just brushing against the banknote rather than pulling it out from under the coins. However, add a small amount of sticky saliva to your finger and the extra friction ensures that the banknote is whipped away every time.

MATCHSTICK MAYHEM

TEN WAYS TO WIN WITH MATCHES

THE AMAZING HISTORY OF THE MODERN MATCH

The ability to create fire is essential to our survival. In the past our ancestors made fire with the heat from a rapidly rotating stick or by striking steel against flint. It was hard and often unrewarding work. Then, in the nineteenth century, an astonishing invention allowed people to effortlessly light up their lives with the simple flick of a wrist. Over the next few pages we will be exploring the fascinating, weird and often downright terrifying events that led to the creation of the modern match. It is a story of alchemists, urine and murder. A story that I have creativity entitled 'A Four-Part History of the Modern Match'.

HORSING AROUND

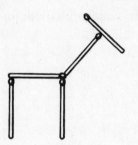

Place five matches on a piece of paper to create a horse looking to the right, like this.

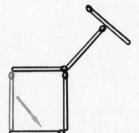

Now challenge your friend to move just one match and make the horse look to the left. To win the bet, first move the horse's back leg through ninety degrees . . .

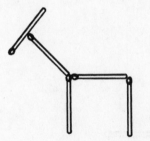

. . . and then just turn the paper around!

Whilst performing this bit, entertain your friends by telling them that horses can lock their legs and sleep standing up, which is handy, because it means that they can escape more quickly if they are attacked.

SQUARE-DANCING

Arrange four matches like this and challenge your friend to create a square by moving just one match.

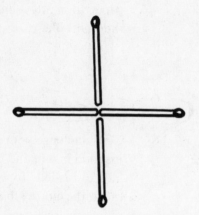

To win the bet, move one of the matches to create a tiny square in the centre!

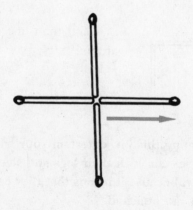

EQUILATERAL

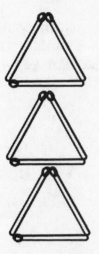

Arrange nine matches like this.

Now challenge your friend to move three matches and make four equilateral triangles. Oh, and none of the matches can overlap one another.

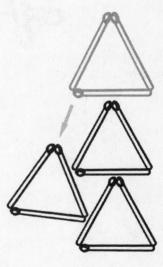

To win the bet, take the three matches that make up the top triangle, and move them to make a new triangle that touches the remaining two triangles, like this.

A TOUCHING PUZZLE

Place six matches on a table and challenge your friend to arrange them in such a way that each match is touching all of the other matches. After they have struggled, arrange the matches like this.

THE HISTORY OF THE MATCH, PART ONE: LIGHT-BRINGING SLAVES

The earliest mention of matches occurs in an ancient Chinese manuscript entitled *Records of the Unworldly and the Strange*. This remarkable document was produced in AD 950 and describes how sticks of sulphur-impregnated pinewood would ignite when placed close to a flame. Referred to as 'light-bringing slaves', these sticks were used in night-time emergencies to instantly create a bright light.

IMPOSSIBLE GLASS

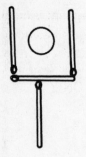

Arrange four matches to represent a wine glass, and place a coin inside the glass. Now challenge your friend to move just two of the matches and end up with the coin outside the glass.

The answer is easy when you know how. First of all, slide the horizontal match to the left like this.

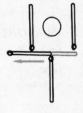

And then take this match and place it here.

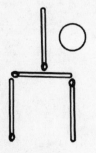

Now the coin is outside the glass and you have won the bet!

IT'S A DOG'S LIFE

Use thirteen matches to create this dog, and then add a small piece of paper to the dog to create an eye. Next, challenge your friend to make the dog look in the opposite direction by moving just two matches and the piece of paper.

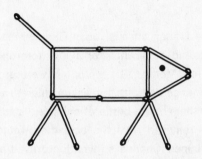

To win the bet, just take the two matches that make up the head, and the piece of paper, and move them like this.

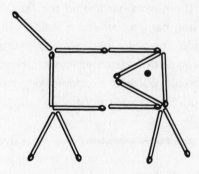

THE HISTORY OF THE MATCH, PART TWO: FRICTION LIGHTS

In 1805, the French chemist Jean Chancel manufactured a primitive, and somewhat terrifying, forerunner of the modern match. Members of the public were provided with wooden splints coated with potassium chlorate and encouraged to dip them into a bottle of sulphuric acid. When the sticks were removed from the acid they would suddenly burst into flames. Chancel's invention proved popular but impractical, with the acid frequently leaking from the bottle and burning people's skin.

In 1826, Englishman John Walker modified Chancel's formula and created sulphur-infused sticks that burst into life when they were rubbed on sandpaper. Although Walker's 'friction lights' eliminated the terrible problems associated with carrying around a leaky bottle of highly corrosive sulphuric acid, his matches emitted noxious smells and frequently fragmented into a torrent of tiny fireballs. As a result, Walker's groundbreaking invention was banned in both France and Germany.

SINK OR SWIM

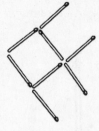

Arrange eight matches to create a fish swimming along to the left. Now challenge your friend to move just three of the matches and make the fish swim in the opposite direction.

To win the bet, just move this match.

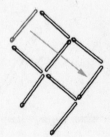

And this one.

And finally move this match. Now the fish is swimming to the right!

EQUATION TIME

Arrange seven matches to make this equation.

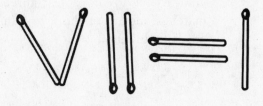

Now challenge your friend to move just one match and make the equation correct. To win the bet, move this match and now everything is fine because the square root of one is one!

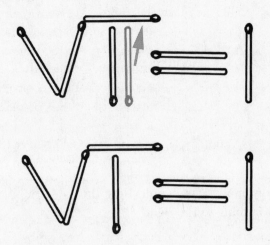

THE HISTORY OF THE MATCH, PART THREE:
FROM URINE TO EUREKA

In 1669, the German alchemist Hennig Brand was busy trying to transform lead into gold by boiling down urine and then heating up the residues. At one point during his experimentation, a glowing liquid dripped out of his furnace and spontaneously burst into flames. Intrigued, Brand examined the liquid and accidentally discovered the substance that would ultimately lead to the invention of the modern match – phosphorus.

For the next 150 years scientists failed to realize that the relationship between phosphorus and fire was a match made in heaven. In 1830, however, French chemist Charles Sauria eventually made the connection and developed the world's first phosphorous match. Although popular, Sauria's invention was still a health and safety nightmare, not least because the matches ignited when they rubbed against almost any rough surface, including trousers. In the 1840s all of this changed when Swedish scientist Gustaf Erik Pasch created a match that ignited only when it was rubbed against a special friction strip on the box. Voilà, the modern-day safety match was born and the future seemed bright. However, as was often the case in the heady world of matchmaking, all was not as it appeared.

SQUARE THINKING

Place twelve matches on a table like this.

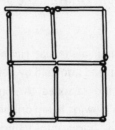

Next, challenge your friend to move just two matches and end up with seven squares. To win the bet, move these two matches . . .

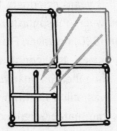

. . . and you have created seven squares!

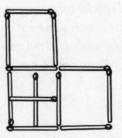

PYRAMID POWER

Place six matches on a table and challenge your friend to arrange them so that they form four equilateral triangles. Explain that they are not allowed to break the matches, and none of the matches can overlap another.

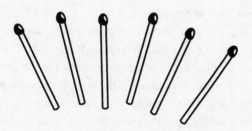

To win the bet simply form a pyramid, like this.

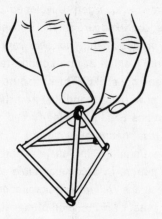

THE HISTORY OF THE MATCH, PART FOUR: SUICIDE AND STRIKES

Phosphorous matches proved a big hit, and by the turn of the last century European and American factories were producing trillions of matches each year. Unfortunately, problems soon emerged.

Firstly, the phosphorus scraped from a single pack of matches contained enough poison to commit suicide or murder. This problem was exacerbated by the then common belief that soaking match heads in brandy resulted in a powerful aphrodisiac. Almost everyone who experimented with this unusual approach to promoting passion lost their life.

Secondly, the match factories had appalling working conditions, and relied on child labour and a poorly paid female workforce who often developed severe health problems caused by exposure to the phosphorus. Thirdly, the production process itself was also very hazardous. In 1888, 1400 match women at one London factory had had enough and went on strike. Their dispute was reported in the national newspapers and inspired the formation of trade unions across Britain. It also forced manufacturers to develop a less dangerous match, and in 1910 the Diamond Match Company in America patented the first non-poisonous match. In a commendable act of altruism, the then US President William Taft persuaded the company to release their patent for the good of mankind.

And so there you have it. Next time you strike one of the half a trillion matches that are used each year, or carry out a match-based bet, spare a thought for those who suffered so that you can safely conjure up fire whenever you want.

OUTSIDE THE BOX

TEN WAYS TO WIN WITH
LATERAL THINKING

AMAZING FACTS ABOUT YOUR BRAIN

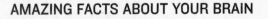 Your brain represents only about 2 per cent of your weight, but contains an amazing 86 billion brain cells and uses roughly 20 per cent of your energy.

☞ Information moves through your brain at a remarkable 260 miles per hour, which is faster than a Formula One racing car.

☞ The pathologist who carried out Albert Einstein's autopsy discovered that the genius's brain was 10 per cent smaller than average. Oh, and he then kept the brain in a jar in his basement for forty years.

☞ The brain has no pain receptors, which explains why brain surgeons can operate on people when they are fully awake.

☞ When surgeons remove half of the brain it has almost no effect on a person's personality or memory.

SIX IN A ROW

Place six glasses in a row and fill the first three with liquid.

Challenge your friend to rearrange the glasses like this . . . but they can only touch *one glass*.

To win the bet, simply pick up Glass 2 and pour the liquid from that glass into Glass 5 . . .

. . . then put Glass 2 back into position and you have won the bet!

THE BIG DROP

Take a toilet roll tube and explain that the bet is to drop it so that it lands standing up on its end. Your friend will fail every time.

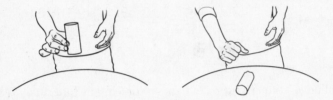

To win the bet, simply drop the tube on its side – it will bounce and land on its end!

The bet works because the toilet roll tube will almost always bounce when it's dropped. When you drop it on its end, it bounces and lands on its side. However, drop it on its side and it will bounce and land on its end.

Why does the tube bounce? If you were to film it hitting the table, and then massively slow down the film, you would see the tube becoming a bit squished as it hits the surface of the table, in the same way that you can feel a ball pushing back against your hand when you squeeze it. So the compressed tube pushes back against the table in an attempt to revert to its original shape. This, in turn, pushes the tube back into the air, and that is why it bounces!

FIVE SURPRISING FACTS ABOUT TOILET ROLLS

☞ 70 per cent of the world's population doesn't use toilet paper.

☞ People use an average of eight sheets of paper per toilet use, which adds up to a hundred rolls of toilet paper each year.

☞ About 380 trees will be cut down to make all of the toilet paper that you will use during your life.

☞ The Romans used a cloth-ended stick instead of toilet paper – hence the origin of the phrase 'getting hold of the wrong end of the stick'.

☞ American talk-show host Johnny Carson once accidentally caused a toilet paper shortage by announcing that there was an acute shortage of toilet paper. The following day viewers bought up every roll they could find, creating a genuine shortage.

PICK ME UP

This bet involves two straws. Cut one straw in half and fold the other in two. Create a pyramid by balancing the folded straw against the tip of one of the halves, and then challenge your friend to pick up the pyramid using the other half-straw.

To win the bet, carefully place the straw inside the top of the pyramid and gently push it against the folded straw. The other half-straw will drop forward onto the straw that you are holding. Finally, lock the half-straw that has just fallen forward under the point of the 'V' of the folded straw, and you can pick everything up.

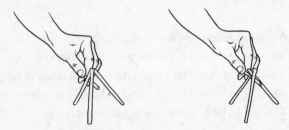

The oldest known drinking straw dates back to 3,000 BC and was discovered in a Sumerian tomb. It consisted of a gold tube inlaid with precious blue stones.

THE IMPOSSIBLE TRIANGLE

Arrange ten coins into a triangle like this.

Now ask your friend to reverse the direction of the triangle by moving just three of the coins. The secret is simple. Take away these three coins.

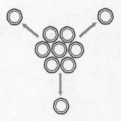

Place two of the coins at the base of the new triangle . . .

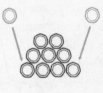

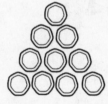

. . . and then the third coin at the top of the new triangle.

ON THE BUSES

Say to your friend, 'Imagine that you are the driver of a bus. At the start of your journey your bus is empty. Then you pick up four passengers. At the next stop two of the passengers get off the bus and another one gets on. Finally, at the next stop two more passengers get on the bus. What is the name of the bus driver?'

When your friend gives up, remind them that you said that they were the driver of the bus, and so the answer is their name!

KNOCK ON WOOD

Bet your friend that they can't sit under a table while you knock on the table three times. When they accept the bet, have them sit under the table, then knock on it twice, and walk away. At some point they will have to come out from under the table and you will have won the bet.

No one knows for sure why knocking on wood is seen as a way of attracting good luck. Some historians believe that the tradition comes from the ancient pagans, who believed that contact with wood evoked the help of the benevolent tree spirits. However, the earliest documented reference to knocking on wood only dates back to 1905, and occurs in a children's chasing game called 'Tiggy-touch-wood'. During the game, one player – called Tiggy – stands in the middle of an area, and the other players touch something wooden (think door, table or fence). One of the players then leaves the safety of their wood and runs across to another piece of wood, and if Tiggy manages to touch them during the run they must take Tiggy's place.

So there we go. Maybe it's an ancient ritual with deep spiritual meaning, or maybe it just comes from Tiggy-touch-wood. One day we hope that researchers will settle the issue once and for all. Touch wood.

ODD THINKING

Place ten coins and three glasses on the table, and bet your friend that you can place the ten coins in the glasses and end up with an odd number of coins in each glass.

To win the bet, drop three coins into the first glass, three coins into the second glass and the remaining four coins into the third glass.

Finally, place the glass containing three coins inside the glass containing four coins. Technically, each glass now holds an odd number of coins!

CREATIVE ACCOUNTING

Arrange nine coins like this, ensuring that there are four coins in one row and five coins in the other row.

Challenge your friend to move just one coin and end up with five coins in each row. To win the bet, just pick up a coin from the end of the row containing five coins and place it on top of the coin at the opposite end of the row. Both rows will now have five coins!

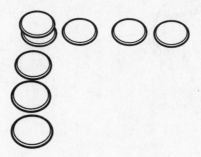

AN OPEN-AND-SHUT CASE

Challenge your friend to drop an empty matchbox onto a table so that it stands on its end. It's almost impossible.

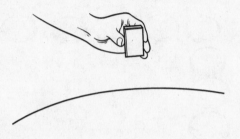

To win the bet, simply open the drawer a tiny amount and then drop the box. When it hits the table, the drawer will close, and the box will stand on its end.

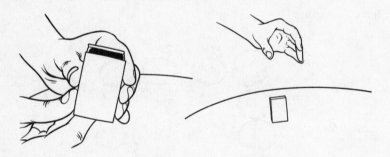

BOTTLE STRAW, STRAW BOTTLE

Challenge your friend to pick up a bottle using just a straw.

The secret is to fold up the bottom third of the straw and place it inside the bottle.

The straw will open up inside, and you will be able to lift the bottle holding just the end of the straw.

Why does this work? Because the weight of the bottle is pushing down on the bent straw, keeping it under tension. This in turn makes the straw rigid and inflexible, and allows you to lift the bottle with the straw.

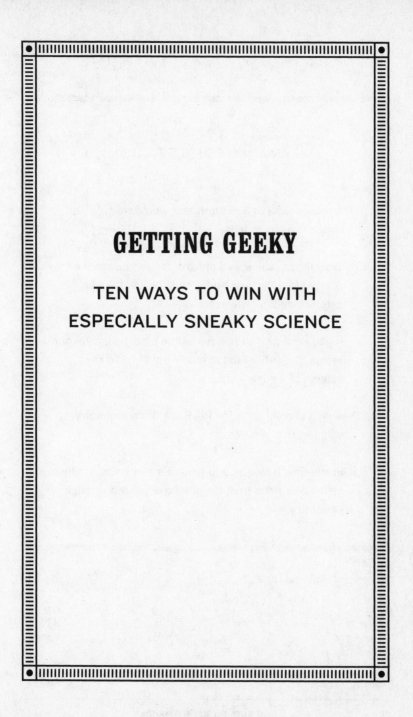

GETTING GEEKY

TEN WAYS TO WIN WITH ESPECIALLY SNEAKY SCIENCE

AMAZING SCIENCE FACTS

☞ A teaspoonful of a neutron star would weigh a colossal 6 billion tons.

☞ Travelling at the speed of light, the journey to the nearest large galaxy, Andromeda, would take an astonishing 2 million years.

☞ If you were able to remove all the empty space in our atoms, the entire human race would fit into the volume of a sugar cube.

☞ A split second after the Big Bang the entire universe was the size of a pea.

☞ In the time it took you to read this sentence, a million billion neutrinos from the sun have passed through your body.

A NOVEL BET

Take two books and weave the pages together. Now challenge your friend to pull the books apart by holding the spines and tugging hard. No matter how hard they try, they will fail and you will win the bet.

Each page of the book has friction against a page above and below it. Since the pages in most books are surprisingly rough, and the combined surface area across all of the pages is huge, a massive amount of friction is created and it's nearly impossible to pull the two books apart by hand. But that is only part of the story – a few years ago a team of French and Canadian physicists discovered a second principle at work. After experimenting with hundreds of carefully prepared test books they realized that the interleaving pages are at a slight angle from the spine. And this matters because when you try to pull the books apart, the pages squeeze together and this massively increases the friction between them.

Without friction, life would be very different. For a start, all knots would automatically untie, cars would remain stationary because their tyres wouldn't grip the road, and everything would slip through your fingers. What's more, walking would be extremely slow and dangerous, and standing on even the slightest of slopes would become a highly treacherous business. On the upside, flights would probably become much, much cheaper, in part because reduced air drag would result in lower fuel consumption, but also because the planes would have no way of stopping when they landed.

A BALANCING ACT

For this bet you need four glasses and three table knives. Place three of the glasses in a triangle, and then challenge your friend to balance three knives on the glasses in such a way that the knives can support the weight of the fourth glass.

To win the bet, place the first and second knives like this . . .

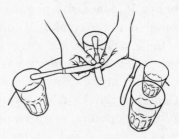

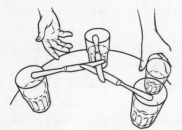

. . . and then place the third knife under the first knife and over the second knife.

The knives will then form a solid platform, and you can balance the fourth glass on it!

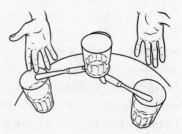

BLOW IN, BLOW OUT

This bet involves a bottle and a pen lid.

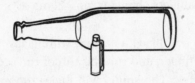

Place the lid in the neck of the bottle, ensuring that the opening of the lid points towards the bottom of the bottle.

Now ask your friend to blow the lid into the bottle. They will blow into the bottle and the lid will come flying out!

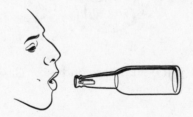

As you blow the air into the bottle it moves around the pen lid and forces out the air in the bottle. The air leaving the bottle then pushes out the pen lid. If you use a plastic bottle, though, and make some holes in the side of the bottle, it will be easy to blow the lid inside it.

PITCH PERFECT

Balance two matches on the rim of a glass. Challenge your friend to make the matches fall into the glass, but without touching the objects, blowing on them, or knocking on the table.

To win the bet, place a second wine glass next to the first one, wet your finger, and rub the rim of the second wine glass until it resonates. The sound will make the matches fall into the wine glass!

Make sure that you hold the second wine glass firmly on the tabletop.

Why does the bet work? When you hold one end of a ruler on the edge of a desk and hit the other end, the ruler will naturally move back and forth at a certain rate. This is the ruler's resonant frequency. It's the same with your finger and the glass. As your finger moves around the rim of the glass it sticks and slides. When you get the movement just right the glass molecules vibrate at their natural frequency and the glass produces the ringing sound. And when this ringing sound hits the second glass it makes the molecules in the second glass move, and these vibrations dislodge the matches.

Of course, it may not feel as if your finger is stopping and starting. However, put some oil around the rim of the glass and your finger will move more smoothly, and the glass won't ring. Conversely, putting some vinegar on your finger beforehand will help remove any dirt or oil, and make it much easier to produce the note.

In the nineteenth century this strange ringing effect was used to create an unusual musical instrument called the glass harmonica. Musicians would rub tuned glass bowls to create different notes, and it was widely believed that the eerie sounds made people go mad. It was later discovered that the musicians were marking the notes with poisonous lead paint, licking their fingers when they played, and therefore ingesting the paint. Saying that, the noise is really annoying.

FINGERTIP CONTROL

This bet involves two forks and a match. Bet your friend that you can balance all three objects on your fingertip. When they accept the bet, carefully push the match between the prongs of the two forks like this.

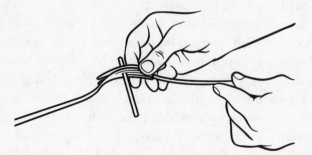

Although it seems impossible, you will then be able to balance the whole set-up on your fingertip.

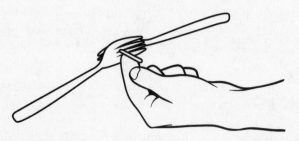

COMPLETELY STATIC

Challenge your friend to balance a straw horizontally on a bottle and then make the straw spin without touching it or blowing on it.

After they have finished struggling, rub the straw on your shirt, balance it on the bottle, and then hold your finger close to the straw. Suddenly the straw will spin around!

Why does it work? Most objects are 'electrically neutral', which means they have an equal amount of positive and negative charge. When you rub the straw on your jumper the straw becomes negatively charged, and when you bring your hand close to the straw the negative charges in your hand are repelled, so your hand becomes positively charged. Unlike charges attract and so the straw moves towards your hand.

Many psychics have used this trick to convince people that they have the power to move objects with the power of their mind. See if you can fool your friends into thinking that you have psychokinetic powers and, if you are successful, ask them if they are interested in helping you form a small cult.

BED OF NAILS

Challenge your friend to place an inflated balloon on an upturned drawing pin without bursting the balloon.

To win the bet, place about twenty drawing pins on a table – amazingly, you can push a balloon onto the drawing pins without it bursting.

When there is only one drawing pin, the entire force on the balloon is focused on that one tip, and so the resulting pressure easily breaks through the rubber of the balloon. However, when you push the balloon onto lots of drawing pins, the same force is distributed across all of the tips and so there is not enough resulting pressure from any single pin to penetrate the rubber.

FULLY CHARGED

Show your friend an empty battery and a full battery, and challenge them to say which is which without putting the batteries into an appliance.

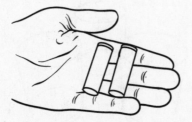

To win the bet, just drop the batteries on a table – the empty battery will bounce much higher than the full battery.

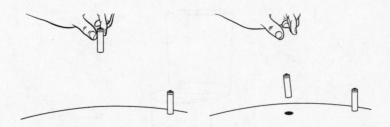

Researchers from Princeton University discovered that this strange phenomenon was caused by the way batteries produce power. The inside of a new battery consists of a layer of zinc wrapped around a brass core. As you use the battery, this zinc slowly changes to zinc oxide, and the links between the particles become more like springs. And it's this springiness that gives the empty battery its bounce.

A TRICKY TOWER

This bet involves three straight-sided glasses. Challenge your friend to make a stack of glasses by balancing them on their rims.

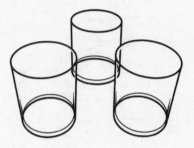

To win the bet, simply stack them up like this.

THE HAPPENING NAPKIN

Take a paper napkin and make a tear on the left-hand side, ensuring that the tear stops about half an inch above the base of the napkin. Do exactly the same on the right-hand side of the napkin. Now ask your friend to hold the two corners of the napkin, and to pull the corners apart so that they are left with three separate pieces.

No matter how carefully they tear, they will always be left with *two* pieces.

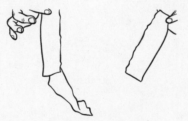

Why does this work? The two tears will be slightly different lengths and so one tear will always give way before the other. The only way of winning the bet is to place the middle part of the napkin in your mouth and then pull on the ends!

WATER WORKS

TEN WAYS TO WIN WITH LIQUID

AMAZING FACTS ABOUT WATER

☞ The great Ancient Greek mathematician Archimedes was fascinated by water, and once famously jumped out of his bath shouting 'Eureka', which is Greek for 'that water was much colder than it looked'.

☞ It takes 150 litres of water to produce a pint of beer.

☞ In 1963, Tanzanian student Erasto Mpemba noticed that, in some circumstances, hot water freezes faster than cold water! The effect is now named after him, and scientists are still uncertain how best to explain this weird phenomenon.

☞ All of the water on Earth arrived in comets and asteroids between 4.5 billion and 3.8 billion years ago.

☞ Since life began, there has been the same amount of water on Earth, and so any glass of water may contain molecules that dinosaurs drank.

THE SEE-SAW

For this bet you need a battery, a ruler and two small cups of water. Place the battery on the table, the ruler on the battery, and balance the cups on either end of the ruler.

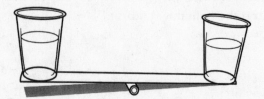

Now challenge your friend to make the see-saw move, but without touching the glasses or the ruler. To win the bet, simply dip your fingers into the water and the see-saw will move!

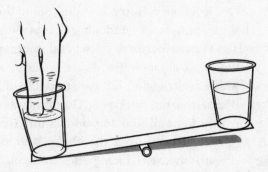

When you put your finger in the water, it increases the level of water in the cup. The deeper the water, the greater the water pressure at the bottom. There's more water pressure acting on the bottom of the cup when you put your finger in it, and so the cup tilts the see-saw.

INSTANT HANDCUFFS

Borrow a banknote from a friend. Ask them to place their hands palm down on the table, and then explain that for the first part of this bet they need to balance two glasses of liquid on the backs of their fingers. Once they are in that position, you pick up the banknote and run!

The legendary Harry Houdini spent his entire life escaping from handcuffs, chains and prisons. However, according to several biographies of the great escapologist, there was one occasion when he struggled for the strangest of reasons. Whilst touring Scotland, Houdini was chained up in a jail cell and the door shut. He quickly freed himself from the chains and started to use concealed lock picks to open the cell door. Houdini struggled for over two hours but simply couldn't open the door. Bathed in sweat and exhausted, he eventually fell against the door. The door swung open and Houdini discovered that it hadn't been locked in the first place! All along, he had been trapped by his own mind.

ALL CHANGE

Draw an arrow on a piece of paper, and then challenge your friend to reverse the direction of the arrow without touching the paper.

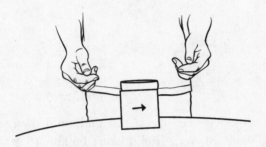

To win the bet, just slide a glass of water in front of the paper and the arrow will appear to reverse direction.

THE UNDRINKABLE DRINK

Tell your friend you're going to place their drink on the table in such a way that they won't be able to drink it. To win the bet, place a thin piece of card over their drink and carefully turn the glass upside down (holding the card in place!).

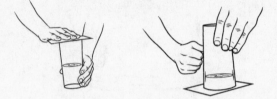

Next, put the entire set-up on the table and then carefully slide away the card. Your friend won't be able to get to their drink, and when they lift the glass the liquid will go everywhere!

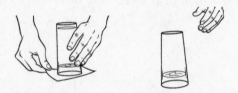

This bet works best with a light, flexible, waterproof piece of card.

Press the card onto the glass as you turn it over.

Use a glass with a relatively large mouth and small base.

This bet is all to do with air pressure. Air pressure is pushing up on the card from below, and the weight of the water is pushing down on the card from above. The force from the air pressure counteracts the force from the water, and the card stays exactly where it is.

EVERY PENNY COUNTS

Fill a wine glass to the brim with water and ask your friend how many pennies you can drop into the glass before the liquid starts to run down the outside.

They will guess maybe one or two coins. In fact, amazingly, you can drop in at least ten pennies without spilling a drop.

The water molecules on the surface of the water cling together very strongly – this is known as surface tension. When you add the pennies the displaced water rises and forms a dome over the rim because the surface of the water stretches. However, add too many pennies and the surface tension won't be strong enough, and the water will start to run down the side of the glass. If you add detergent to the water the surface tension will be much lower, and far fewer pennies can be placed in the glass before it starts to spill.

DOWN IN ONE

Place a straw in a bottle and tell your friend that you can move half of the liquid from the bottle into a glass, but without moving the bottle or sucking on the straw.

To win the bet, simply place your lips around the top of the bottle and blow. The air pressure will force the liquid through the straw and into the glass!

In 1888, Marvin Chester Stone, an American, invented the modern drinking straw. Stone wrapped paper around a pencil, slid the tube off the pencil, and applied glue to the side of the tube. These early straws were about eight inches long and very narrow, much like a modern-day cocktail straw. Stone's simple invention has improved millions of lives because straws help prevent acidic soft drinks coming into direct contact with people's teeth, and so significantly reduce tooth decay and cavities.

Unlike many nineteenth-century industrialists, Stone cared deeply about his workers. He provided them with a well-stocked library, a music room and a dance hall, and constructed tenement houses for Washington's African American residents.

IN THE CAN

Bet your friend that you are able to balance an empty drink can on its rim.

When your friend accepts the bet, place about 100 milli-litres of water in the can and you will find that you can balance it on its rim. In fact, if you give the can a gentle tap, it will roll around the table on its rim!

When you have a can of liquid, its centre of gravity is roughly in the middle of the liquid. As a result, a can containing lots of liquid has a relatively high centre of gravity. When you attempt to balance the can on its rim, the centre of gravity won't be in line with where the rim touches the table, and the can will topple over. When you pour away some of the liquid, however, you lower the centre of gravity, and at some point the can's centre of gravity will be directly above where the rim touches the table. Now the can will balance at a seemingly impossible angle.

A FANTASTIC FLOTATION

Fill a glass with water and challenge your friend to float a paper clip on top of the water. Every time they place a paper clip in the glass it will sink to the bottom.

To win the bet, bend one paper clip into an 'L' shape, and then balance another paper clip on the arm of the 'L'.

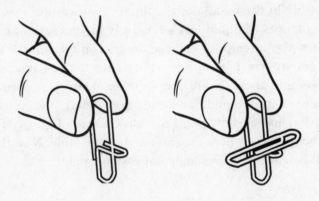

Finally, carefully place the entire arrangement on the top of the water. Amazingly, the paper clip will float.

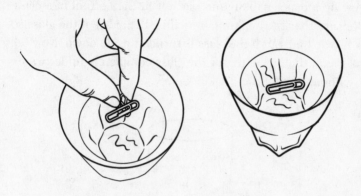

The bet works because the molecules on the top of the water are held strongly together by surface tension, forming a thin film. This film can support very light objects, provided that they don't disturb the tension. If people use their hands to place the paper clips in the water, the oil on their fingers disturbs the tension. Use an L-shaped paper clip, however, and the tension remains intact.

And if you want to win the bet even when your friend knows how to put in the paper clips, secretly add a drop of liquid soap to the water. The soap will break up the surface tension, and the soapy water won't support a paper clip no matter how carefully it's placed in the glass!

THE DIVING BELL

Screw up a paper napkin and place it in the bottom of a glass.
Make sure that the napkin is touching the sides of the glass so
that it won't fall out if the glass is turned upside down. Now tell
your friend that you can put the glass completely under water,
but without getting the napkin wet.

To win the bet, push the glass into a bowl of water mouth first.
The air pressure will stop the water getting into the glass and
the napkin will remain completely dry!

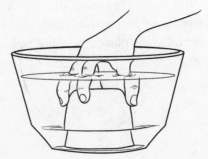

HALF FULL OR HALF EMPTY?

Fill a straight-sided glass three-quarters full of water. Then challenge your friend to pour some of it out until they are left with exactly half a glass of water.

To win the bet, pour the water until there's a straight line between the rim and the base of the glass – then you have exactly half a glass of water.

KITCHEN CAPERS

TEN WAYS TO WIN WITH FOOD

AMAZING FACTS ABOUT FOOD

☞ Honey tastes nice, but is actually made from nectar and bee vomit.

☞ There are over 7,000 varieties of apples, and so if you tried a new one every day, it would take twenty years to get through them all.

☞ The shiny coating often used on sweets is made from the bodily excretions of an Asian beetle.

☞ Around AD 250 the Mayans and the Aztecs used cocoa beans as currency.

☞ Archaeological evidence suggests that soup was first eaten around 6,000 BC, and was made from hippopotamus.

THE GREAT SPAGHETTI CHALLENGE

Ask someone to hold the ends of a piece of uncooked spaghetti like this . . .

. . . and now challenge them to bend the spaghetti and break it into just *two* pieces. It sounds simple, but they will always end up with more than two pieces, and you will win the bet!

This bet has baffled many great minds, including the bongo-playing scientist Richard Feynman. In 2005 two French physicists solved the mystery using high-speed cameras, lots of equations and a trolleyful of spaghetti. In their report, 'Fragmentation of Rods by Cascading Cracks: Why Spaghetti Does Not Break in Half', they explain how the first break creates a fast-moving shock wave that travels along the two newly formed spaghetti pieces and causes additional breaks.

ORANGE DELIGHT

This bet involves a glass and an orange. Place the glass on the table and challenge your friend to balance the orange on the top of the glass.

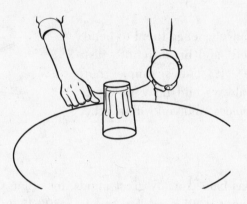

When they do this . . .

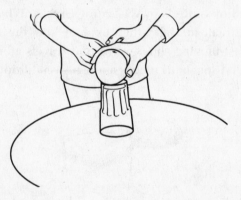

. . . explain that you have won the bet because they have placed the orange on the *bottom* of the glass!

THE PERFECT ICEBREAKER

Place an ice cube in a drink and challenge your friend to remove the cube using a piece of thread.

To win the bet, place the end of the thread on the ice cube and pour some salt onto it. After about a minute you will be able to lift the cube out of the drink using just the thread.

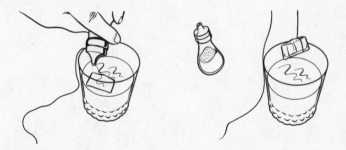

Salt lowers the freezing point of water. 'But how does this happen?' I hear you ask. Well, when water is a liquid, its molecules whizz around quite quickly and keep their distance from one another. As you cool the water down, some of the energy needed for the aforementioned whizzing is removed, and the molecules move more slowly. And when you get to very low temperatures, the water molecules move so slowly that they get close to one another and eventually link together to form solid ice. If you add salt to the water, the salt molecules get in the way of the linking-up, and so the temperature has to be even lower before the mixture becomes a solid. When you sprinkled the salt on the ice you lowered its freezing point, and so turned ice back into liquid water. However, after a few moments the surrounding ice water refroze, trapping the thread in the ice.

The same principle explains why it's good to sprinkle salt on a road when the weather is wet and chilly. The salt lowers the freezing point of rain and makes the water less likely to turn into treacherous ice. If the temperature is extremely low (think −30°C) the salt won't be effective, and you have to use a chemical called sodium acetate. This is also the chemical used to flavour salt and vinegar crisps. Which perhaps explains why they melt in your mouth.

EGG-STRAORDINARY

Show your friend that you can balance an egg on its end and ask them to do the same. They won't be able to do it because they don't know the secret.

Before you start, pour a small pile of salt on the table, place the egg on the salt and then blow most of the pile away. The egg will remain balanced on just a few grains of salt.

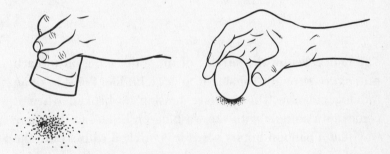

Eggs naturally rest on their side because then their centre of gravity is as low as possible. However, it only takes a few grains of salt to cheat gravity by providing enough friction to support the egg in an upright position.

RUN AWAY

Sprinkle some pepper into a bowl of water and challenge your friend to make the pepper move towards the edge of the bowl.

To win the bet, simply place some washing-up liquid on your fingertip and touch the water. The pepper will magically move away towards the edge of the bowl.

The molecules on the surface of the water cling on to each other very strongly, causing it to act a bit like the skin of an inflated balloon. This 'surface tension' is broken when it comes into contact with the washing-up liquid, in the same way that a balloon bursts when it is pricked with a pin. The water molecules then rush to the sides of the bowl, taking the pepper with them.

STRAW THROUGH POTATO

Bet your friend that you can push a plastic straw through a potato.

When your friend accepts the bet, hold the potato between your thumb and fingers, making sure that your hand isn't behind the potato. Next, hold the straw in your other hand, about two-thirds of the way up

Finally, quickly stab the straw into the narrow end of the potato and you will find that it goes all the way through. Sometimes it helps to hold your thumb over the top end of the straw, or fold the end of the straw over.

The end of the plastic straw has a very small surface area and so the force you apply when you push the straw is concentrated in a small area. It's really important, though, to keep the straw straight when you stab the potato.

PEPPER PICK-UP

Sprinkle some salt and pepper on a plate, mix it all up, and then challenge your friend to pick up only the pepper.

To win the bet, simply inflate a balloon, rub it on your T-shirt or jumper, and place the balloon over the plate. Static electricity will make the pepper jump up onto the balloon, leaving the salt on the plate.

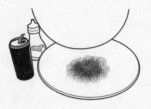

Why does this work? It's our old friend, Mr Static Electricity, at work again. When you rub the balloon on your jumper, negatively charged electrons move from your jumper to the balloon, giving the balloon a negative charge. Then, when you bring the balloon close to the salt and pepper, the negatively charged balloon makes negatively charged electrons on the salt and pepper move away (like charges repel and unlike charges attract), leaving the salt and pepper positively charged. The positive salt and pepper are then attracted to the negative balloon. However, the grains of salt are relatively heavy and so it's harder for them to move, whereas the lighter pepper can more easily leap up onto the balloon.

BLOW ON MY CHERRY

Place a cherry tomato in a small wine glass, and then challenge your friend to remove the tomato without touching it or the glass.

To win the bet, blow directly into the glass as hard as you can. The cherry tomato will jump right out!

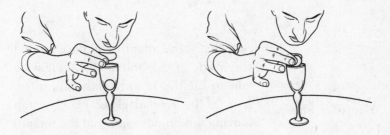

It's all down to air pressure. When you blow into the wine glass, the tapering shape of the glass means that the air pressure at the bottom of the glass is increased. This air then tries to escape by moving back up, and this rapid movement of air pushes the cherry tomato out of the glass.

IN A SPIN

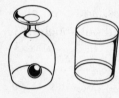

This bet involves a brandy glass, a small tomato and a second glass. Turn the brandy glass upside down and place it over the tomato. Now challenge your friend to move the tomato into the second glass, but they are only allowed to hold the base of the brandy glass.

To win the bet, hold the base of the brandy glass, lift the glass a tiny amount off the table, and move the glass in a circle. When you are moving it quite quickly, touch the tomato with the inside of the brandy glass.

Amazingly, the tomato will move around the inside of the brandy glass, allowing you to lift the brandy glass and move it over the second glass. Finally, stop moving the brandy glass and the tomato will fall out into the second glass.

Ask your friend why this bet works and they will probably mutter something about centrifugal force. They are wrong. In fact, physicists are not at all keen on the term 'centrifugal force' (Latin for 'fleeing from the centre'), with some arguing that the term should be banned and the people using it shot. According to Newton's law of motion, the tomato is being acted upon by a 'centripetal force'. So now you know.

LEMON-AID

Place a lemon in a glass of water. Next, challenge your friend to take a coin from their pocket and balance it on the lemon.

Tell them that you will keep the coin if it falls into the water. It sounds simple, but whenever they place a coin on the lemon, the lemon will roll over and the coin will fall into the water.

Lemons are high in vitamin C and help prevent scurvy. The demand for scurvy-preventing lemons peaked during the 1849 California Gold Rush, when malnourished miners would pay vast amounts of money for a single lemon. As a result, the number of lemon trees in California rocketed and even today the state's citrus-based business is valued at more than $1 billion annually.

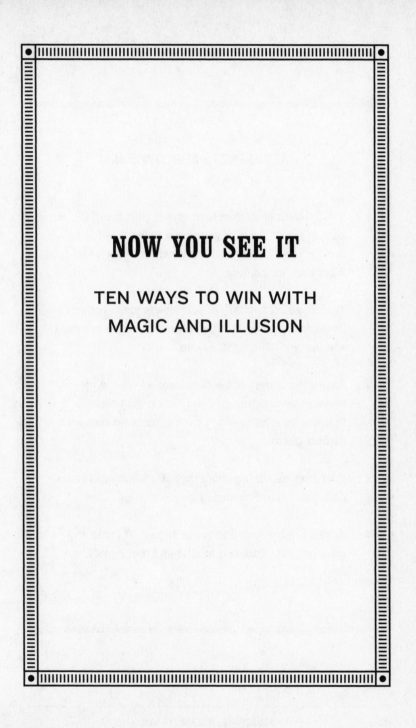

NOW YOU SEE IT

TEN WAYS TO WIN WITH
MAGIC AND ILLUSION

AMAZING FACTS ABOUT VISION

☞ Vision is our most dominant sense, with about 30 per cent of the neurons in your brain being devoted to seeing, compared to just 8 per cent for touch and 2 per cent for hearing.

☞ The image on the back of your eye is actually upside down, but your brain turns it around and allows you to see the world the right way up.

☞ Each of your eyes has a blind spot where the optic nerve attaches, but you don't notice the holes because your brain fills in each eye's blind spot with its best guess.

☞ Your eyes can detect more than 10 million colours but only about thirty shades of grey.

☞ Babies are hardwired to prefer to look at faces and are especially attracted to anything that looks like eyes.

LINE THEM UP

Show this picture to your friend and tell them that the horizontal lines are straight. When they don't believe you, use a ruler to prove that you're right.

This illusion was first reported by psychologist Professor Richard Gregory in 1979. Gregory was studying visual perception in Bristol, and a member of his team saw the illusion in the tiling on the wall of a local cafe. Ever since then it has been referred to as the 'cafe wall' illusion.

MONKEYING AROUND

Bet your friend that you can show them something that no human has ever seen before, nor will ever see again. When they accept the bet, take a monkey nut out of your pocket and open it. No human has ever seen that particular nut before. Next, pop it into your mouth and eat it. Now no human will ever see it again!

Peanuts are not nuts but rather a type of legume – that is, a plant with seeds that grow inside pods (think peas or beans). Whereas nuts grow on trees, peanuts grow underground.

THE QUEEN IS AMUSED

Tell your friend that you can make the portrait on a banknote smile. When they accept the bet, take any banknote with a portrait on it (try a ten-pound note*) and fold the note over along the middle of the person's nose. Next, put a second crease, in the opposite direction, through each of the portrait's eyes, so that you end up with a zigzag banknote.

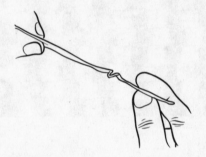

When you tip the note away from you the person in the portrait will smile, and when you tip it towards you they will frown.

* Or, in the U.S., a $5 bill.

THE HAT-TRICK

Place a coin on a table heads up and cover it with a hat. Tell your friend that you can make the coin turn over, but without touching the hat. Next, click your fingers and announce that the coin has flipped over. When your friend picks up the hat to see if you are right, quickly reach forward and turn the coin over. You have won the bet!

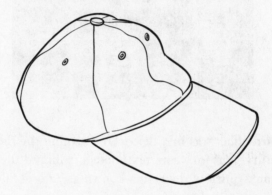

GOING DOTTY

Show your friend this page and ask them to count the black dots. They will be there forever!

This weird effect was first discovered around the turn of the last century, and for years textbooks attributed the illusion to a strange quirk of the retina known as 'lateral inhibition'. The bad news is that this explanation is very complicated. The much better news is that we don't have to concern ourselves with the explanation because it was recently shown to be complete nonsense. Some researchers now believe that the illusion is due to 'S1 type simple cells' in the retina, but give it a couple of years and that will probably be shown to be wrong too. Quite frankly, no one really knows what's going on. If you have any good ideas, jot them down on a postcard, mark it, 'Solution to grid illusion: you know, the one where you see the dots in the gaps', and send it to your nearest psychology department.

THE MISSING PIECE

Cut a rectangular piece of paper into five parts like this.

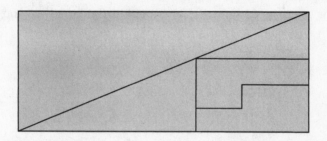

Reassemble them in front of your friend, and announce that you will assemble the rectangle again, but this time one part of it will magically disappear. When your friend accepts the bet, just exchange the two triangles, put the other pieces back like this, and now one square has vanished.

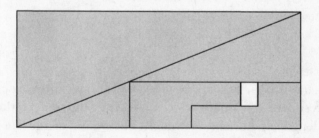

Actually, the second rectangle isn't perfect. Instead, there are several irregularities which, when they are all added up, account for the missing square.

A TALL DRINK

Bet your friend that the circumference of a pint glass is actually twice the height of the glass. When they don't believe you, use a piece of string or a napkin to show that you are right.

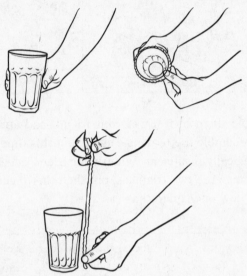

This bet works, in part, because we all have a tendency to overestimate the length of vertical things and underestimate the length of horizontal things. The width of the glass is horizontal and the height is vertical, and so we tend to think that it is narrower and taller than it actually is. The illusion does, however, have an upside. Researchers filmed people walking up some steps. Some of the time the front of the steps had horizontal lines painted on them, and some of the time they had vertical lines. The vertical lines made people overestimate the height of a step, which meant that they were less likely to trip over it.

FIND THE QUEEN

This bet involves a paper clip and five playing cards. One of the playing cards should be a queen. Place the queen in the middle position and spread the playing cards out. Show the playing cards to your friend, then turn your hand over and ask your friend to place the paper clip on the queen.

The way you're holding the cards means that they will clip the paperclip around all of them and, because the back of the queen lines up with the face of the front card, when you turn the playing cards back around they'll see that they have placed the paper clip on the front playing card, and you will win the bet.

THE EYES HAVE IT

Show your friend this page and ask them to read the sentence in the box.

> Quirkology, the YouTube
> channel that plays with
> with your mind.

They will probably say 'Quirkology, the YouTube channel that plays with your mind'. In fact, the box contains a repetition of the word 'with'.

Your brain would have to be the size of a planet to be able to make sense of the constant stream of stuff that it receives from your eyes. Instead, without you knowing it, your brain cuts corners by relying on your past experience to double-guess what's going on around you. For instance, if you see just three legs of a chair, you instantly assume that there is a fourth leg that you can't see, because almost all of the chairs you have seen in the past have four legs. Most of the time your brain is right to make these shortcuts and everything is hunky-dory. However, once in a while you come across something that you rarely see – such as a sentence with two 'with's – and suddenly you fail to to see what is right in front of your eyes.

MIND GAMES

Tell your friend that you can make them say the word seven.

Then say, 'What's two plus two?'

They will reply 'four'.

Then ask, 'What's three plus three?'

They will say 'six', and then you reply: 'I won the bet, because you said six.'

They will answer, 'But you said you would make me say seven.'

And then you really have won the bet.

BOTTOMS UP

Half fill two champagne glasses.

Now tell your friend that all of the liquid from one glass will fit into the other. The shape of the champagne glasses creates an optical illusion, and the glasses look as if they contain loads of liquid. When your friend accepts the bet, just pour the liquid from one glass into the other and you win the bet.

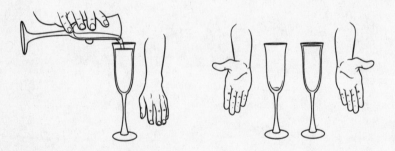

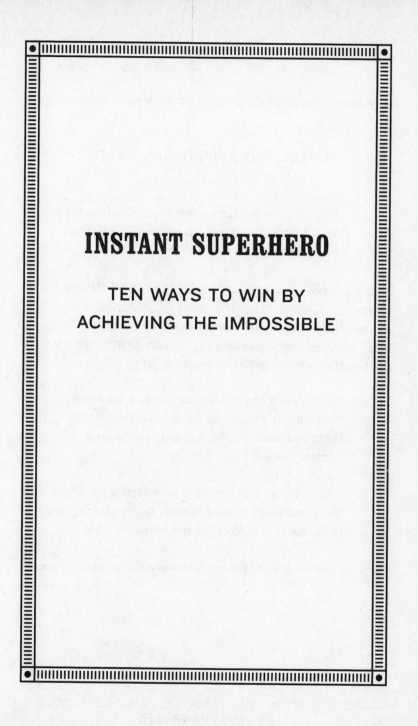

INSTANT SUPERHERO

TEN WAYS TO WIN BY
ACHIEVING THE IMPOSSIBLE

AMAZING FACTS ABOUT SUPERHEROES

☞ In the 1940s there was a comic book superhero called the Green Lama who was a practising Buddhist and could reincarnate at will.

☞ Marvel's 'Wolverine' was going to be called 'Badger'.

☞ The Incredible Hulk was originally grey. It was difficult to print the same shade of grey consistently, however, and so he was soon rebranded as green.

☞ Batman's real name, Bruce Wayne, was inspired by two historical figures: the Scottish king Robert the Bruce and American Revolutionary war general Anthony Wayne.

☞ William Marston invented the lie-detecting polygraph and also created Wonder Woman, thus explaining why her Golden Lasso forces people to tell the truth.

HOW TO CLIMB THROUGH A POSTCARD

Bet your friend that you can climb through a postcard. When they accept the bet, fold the card in half and cut along these vertical lines, making sure that you cut both sides of the fold.

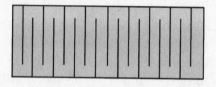

Then unfold the postcard and cut along the dotted line, being careful not to cut through the ends of the card.

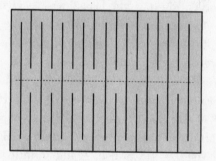

Now, when you carefully pull on the ends it will open out to form a ring that you can climb through.

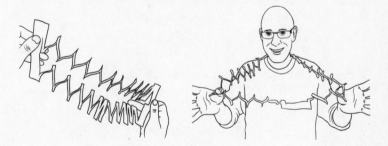

The world's first postcard was created and sent by Englishman Theodore Hook in 1840. Hook addressed the card to himself, and it was meant as a practical joke on the postal service because it depicts postal workers as mindless scribes. In 2002, Hook's groundbreaking postcard sold for an amazing £31,750.

Theodore Hook also created one of the most amazing bets of the entire nineteenth century. In 1810, Hook bet a friend that within a week he could transform any London house into the most talked-about address in the city. His friend accepted the bet and chose a small house in London's Berners Street as their target.

Hook sent out hundreds of letters requesting deliveries to the house, and within days the house was receiving an endless stream of tradespeople, including sweeps, cake makers, lawyers, priests, fishmongers, shoemakers, and piano tuners. In his next wave of letters Hook invited various dignitaries to tea at the house, resulting in visitations from the Governor of the Bank of England, the Archbishop of Canterbury, and the Lord Mayor of London. This mass of activity created complete chaos, and the police were eventually called to prevent people from visiting the house. Hook monitored the whole affair from the house opposite, delighted that he had won his outrageous bet.

X MARKS THE SPOT

Take a piece of cardboard and place an 'X' on each side.

Tell your friend that you are going to drop the cardboard on a table, and they will win if it lands 'X' side up. Before you drop the cardboard, fold it into an L-shape, and then it will always land on its edge and you will win the bet.

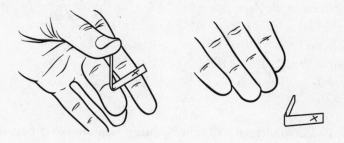

TRAPPED

Put a rubber band over your first and middle fingers, and then use another band to link your fingers together like this.

Now tell your friend that you can move the first band to your third and fourth fingers but without removing the other band. To win the bet, just stretch the band out like this . . .

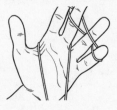

. . . then place your four fingers inside and when you open your hand the band will have jumped across.

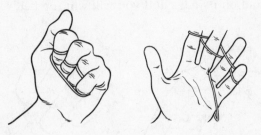

In 1923, American William Spencer was annoyed because his local newspaper tended to fall apart and the pages would blow down the street. Spencer sliced some rubber inner tubes into circular strips, and persuaded local printers to wrap the bands around their newspapers. The scheme worked well and Spencer started to sell his newfangled 'rubber bands' across the region. Today, Spencer's company – Alliance Rubber – manufactures more than 6 million kilograms of rubber bands each year.

KNOT IMPOSSIBLE

Give your friend a piece of rope or string, and challenge them to hold the ends and tie a knot in the string without letting go. When they give up, place the string on the table, cross your arms, then grip the ends of the string and tie a knot by uncrossing your arms.

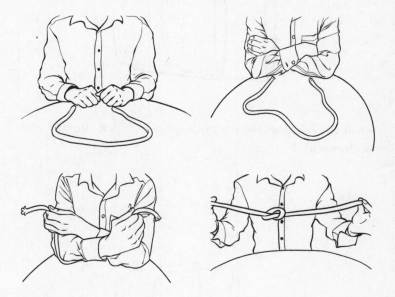

When you fold your arms you are actually tying them in a knot. Then, when you grasp the ends of the rope it becomes an extension of your arms, and when you unfold your arms you transfer the knot from your arms to the rope.

BLOWN APART

Place one plastic cup inside another and challenge your friend to separate the cups without touching them.

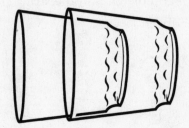

To win the bet, just blow into the area between the two cups and they will fly apart.

THE BIG HOP

Place two chairs in the middle of the floor and tell your friend that you are going to take off your shoes and hop over them.

When your friend accepts the bet, take off your shoes and hop over your shoes!

THE PEN THAT WRITES ANY COLOUR

Bet your friend that you have a pen that can write any colour.

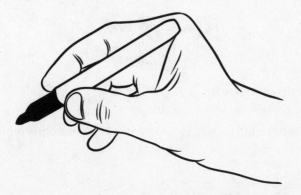

When they accept the bet, ask them to name a colour. If, for example, they say 'red', then simply write the word 'RED'! Your pen can write any colour and so you win the bet.

LINKED AT BIRTH

This bet involves a banknote and two paper clips.

Fold the note into a zigzag and place the paper clips on it like this.

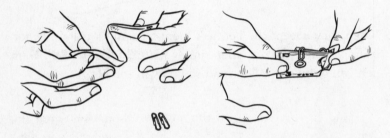

Now tell your friend that you are going to flick the paper clips off the note and when the paper clips land they will be touching one another. You will win the bet, because when you pull the sides of the banknote the two paper clips will fly off and land linked together!

TEA TOWEL TO CHICKEN

Ask your friend if it's possible to transform a tea towel into a chicken. When they say no, lay out a tea towel, roll up each of the shorter sides of the towel until they meet in the centre . . .

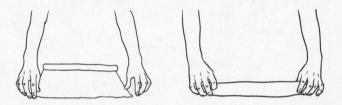

. . . and then fold it in half. Pull out each of the four corners . . .

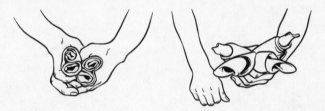

. . . and then grasp two of the corners in one hand and the other two in the other hand. Pull hard and suddenly you have a chicken!

If your friend struggles to see the chicken, explain that highly imaginative people also tend to be very intelligent.

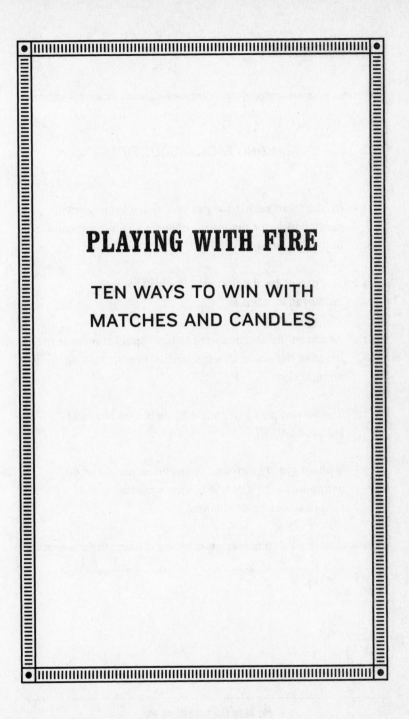

PLAYING WITH FIRE

TEN WAYS TO WIN WITH
MATCHES AND CANDLES

AMAZING FACTS ABOUT FIRE

☞ In Iraq there's a natural gas vent that's been burning continuously for thousands of years and is mentioned in the Old Testament.

☞ The patent for the first ever fire hydrant was destroyed in a fire.

☞ American fire stations used to have spiral staircases because the station horses learned how to walk up straight ones.

☞ The hottest part of a candle flame is light blue and burns at 1,400°C.

☞ Without gravity warm air doesn't rise, and so when astronauts light a candle in space the flame is spherical instead of elliptical.

POP SCIENCE

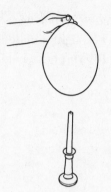

Bet your friend that you can hold an inflated balloon over a candle without bursting it.

To win the bet, place some water in the balloon, blow it up, tie it off, and then gently lower it over the candle. Amazingly, it won't burst.

Place a balloon above a candle and the heat will quickly melt the rubber. However, if the balloon has some water inside then this heat is quickly transferred to the water. Better still, the water requires a large amount of energy to heat up, and so it remains cool for a long time. This, in turn, keeps the balloon cool and helps prevent it from bursting.

HOLDING A LIT MATCH UNDER WATER

Tell your friend that you can hold a lit match under water without it going out. When they accept the bet, light a match and hold it under a glass of water. Technically, you have held a lit match under water!

CANDLE IN THE WIND

For this bet you need a funnel and a candle. Light the candle and challenge your friend to blow it out by blowing from the narrow end of a funnel. Amazingly, no matter how hard they blow they won't be able to do it.

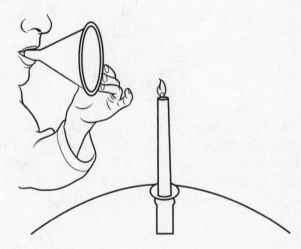

Some scientists think that when you blow into the funnel your breath spreads out along the funnel walls, and very little air makes it to the flame. Other scientists don't have a clue why it works. Either way, if you blow through the wide end of the funnel your breath will be more focused and it will be easy to blow out the candle.

BURN BABY BURN

Make a hole in an *empty* matchbox and put a match vertically into the hole. Place a coin on the matchbox, and then place a second match on the coin and lean it against the top of the upright match. Challenge your friend to remove the coin without touching either of the matches.

To win the bet, light a third match and place it under the centre of the diagonal match. The flame will travel along the diagonal match. At one end it will ignite the upright match and bond the two matches together. At the other end it will cause the match to lift into the air, enabling you to remove the coin!

GLASS-BLOWING

Place a lit candle in front of a bottle, go behind the bottle and tell your friend that you can blow out the candle without touching the bottle or moving from your position.

To win the bet, simply blow. The air currents will move around the bottle, and the candle will be extinguished.

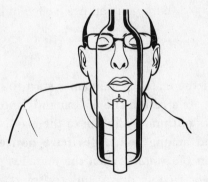

GOING UP

Place a coin on a plate and then pour some water over it. Now challenge your friend to pick up the coin without getting their fingers wet.

To win the bet, put three matches into a piece of cork, place the cork on the water, and light the matches.

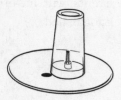

Place a glass over the matches, avoiding the coin. The water will be drawn up into the glass, allowing you to remove the coin. If you don't have a piece of cork you can use a slice of lemon.

When you cover the matches the flames start to heat the air inside the glass. As a result, the air expands and some of it eventually comes out under the rim of the glass. In fact, the more sharp-eyed among you might have noticed the tiny bubbles of air in the water. When the matches go out, the air inside the glass cools down and contracts. As the air contracts it pulls the water into the glass, allowing you to pick up the coin.

A STICKY SOLUTION

For this bet you need two glasses, a match, and some coins. Place one glass over the coins and balance the match between the glasses like this. Challenge your friend to pick up the coins, but without moving the match.

To win the bet, use another match to light the first one and quickly blow it out. Wait a few seconds and the match will stick to the side of the glass. You will then be able to pick up the other glass and grab the coins.

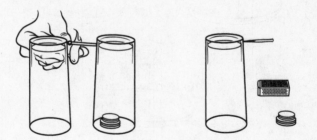

PICK ME UP

Challenge your friend to pick up a glass with an inflated balloon.

To win the bet, carefully drop a lit match into the glass and push the balloon onto the rim of the glass. The match will burn out, sucking the balloon into the glass and allowing you to pick up the glass using the balloon.

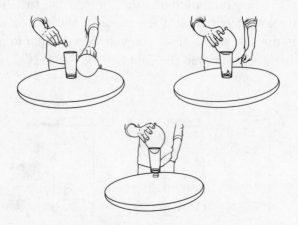

Why does it work? The burning match heats up the air, which then expands, rises up, and starts to escape from the glass. When you place the balloon on the glass and the match goes out, the air left in the glass cools down and contracts, sucking in the balloon and sealing it against the rim of the glass.

LIFT-OFF

Tell your friend that you can turn a teabag into a rocket. For this bet you need a teabag that is folded and stapled at the top.

Cut off the top and bottom of the bag (including the staple), open the bag and empty out the tea. Next, make the teabag into a tube and stand the tube upright on a plate.

Finally, light the top of the tube and it will burn down. Just before it gets to the end, however, the entire teabag will fly into the air like a rocket!

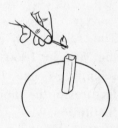

Setting fire to the teabag heats the air inside the tube, and the hot air starts to rise. As the teabag changes into ash it becomes lighter, and eventually the uplift provided by the warm air is enough to raise the teabag. Hot-air balloons work on exactly the same principle and were originally made from giant teabags (I made this last bit up).

WE HAVE IGNITION

Challenge your friend to light a candle, but without touching it with a match or lighter. When they give up, first light the candle with a match.

Now quickly blow out the candle and carefully place the lit match in the smoke emerging from the wick.

The flame will magically travel down the smoke and relight the candle!

The science of candles is fascinating, and in 1860 the great Victorian scientist Michael Faraday devoted six lectures to the topic at London's Royal Institution.

We don't have that kind of time so I'll keep it short. When a candle burns, the heat vaporizes the wax as it travels up the wick.

When you blow out the candle, there's still enough heat in the wick to continue vaporizing the wax, and the resulting vapour drifts up in the smoke. Place a match in the smoke and *voilà*, you ignite the vapour, causing the flame to travel down and relight the candle.

FEELING LUCKY?

For our final bet I thought it would be fun to turn the book itself into a bet.

This is one of my all-time favourite bets, and so I hope that you have a great time with it.

Thanks for playing, and I hope to see you soon on the Quirkology YouTube channel for more quirky bets and mind-boggling illusions.

Hand your friend a die and tell them that they have thirty seconds to . . .

- roll the die,
- add up the numbers on the top and bottom of the die,
- and turn to that page number in this book.

When your friend rolls the die, the top and bottom numbers will add up to seven.

However, there is no page seven in this book, and so you will always win the bet!